J.M. CASIDY

LOVE IS A CHOICE

**The Essential Guide to Winning Your Ex Back, Discover
The Lessons You Can Learn from a Break-Up and Effective
Strategies to Getting Back Together With Your Ex**

Descrierea CIP a Bibliotecii Naționale a României
J.M. CASIDY
   LOVE IS A CHOICE. The Essential Guide to Winning Your
Ex Back, Discover The Lessons You Can Learn from a Break-Up
and Effective Strategies to Getting Back Together With Your Ex /
J.M. Casidy. – Bucharest: Editura My Ebook, 2020
   ISBN

J.M. CASIDY

LOVE IS A CHOICE

**The Essential Guide to Winning Your Ex Back, Discover
The Lessons You Can Learn from a Break-Up and Effective
Strategies to Getting Back Together With Your Ex**

My Ebook Publishing House
Bucharest, 2020

TABLE OF CONTENTS

FOREWORD

Everyone in life has most likely experienced heartbreak at one point or another in their life. This does not change the fact that it is very painful and nobody really wants to go through it. The problem with that is the fact that in order to find love you have to take the chance of losing love.

Some people may feel like their entire life is over if their partner decides to split ways. If you are one of these people you need to understand that there is still hope and that there is a chance that your relationship can be repaired and you can be holding your loved one again in no time at all. Trying to win your ex back is a delicate process and there are some steps that need to be taken in order to ensure that the entire process goes smoothly. In most cases it will not be as simple as simply asking the person to come back because there was obviously a reason they left in the first place. You must remember not to try to rush the process and to let your ex set the pace.

Winning back an ex can be a very difficult process if not done in the correct way. This book will provide you with some helpful information that will guide you in the right direction towards winning back your ex. Continue reading if you are serious about winning back your loved one's heart.

Winning Your Heart Again

How to Turn Your Ex into Yours

CHAPTER 1

RECOVER FROM A BROKEN HEART

Synopsis

The first thing that you are going to need to do if you want to win your ex's heart back is to recover from your own broken heart. You will likely be emotional with a fresh tear on your heart and when you are emotional your decisions may not be as wise as when you have a clear head. It is important to remember that time heals everything, even your heart. You need to keep in mind that everything will get better and you have to truly believe that you will win your ex back someday.

The following chapter will go over the importance of recovering from your broken heart before trying to win back your ex. This chapter will also provide you with some helpful tips that may help to speed up the process a little bit as well as make things easier for you.

Heal Your Heart

As mentioned before, it is extremely important that you heal the wounds of your broken heart before you make any attempts of trying to win back your ex. Chances are that there was an issue in your relationship and that is why you split up in the first place. You need to be able to fix these problems in your relationship if you ever want things to work out. The chances of this happening while you still have fresh wounds on your heart are slim. People can make poor decisions and have illogical though processes while emotional so it is best to give it a little bit of time before trying to jump straight back into the relationship.

You may feel as if the pain will never go away and that you will never be happy again. Do not feel this way! It is understandable that this is a task much easier said than done but it is possible. The pain will eventually fade and the wounds will begin to heal, you just have to give it time.

The following are ten tips that will help you through this process and make it as easy as possible for you.

- **Understand The Reality Of Your Situation:**

It is highly important that you understand that the love that you felt was real, regardless of whether or not it lasted forever. You must not fall into a state where you think it was all fake and the feelings were never real. You need to understand that you were not foolish and that there are just some issues that need to be addresses.

- **Appreciate The Gift Of Love:**

Love is always a gift, even if it doesn't last. You should keep in mind that even if you have lost someone you love, you have experienced something wonderful that many people have not found and may not ever find at all. Appreciating that life blessed you with love, even if it was brief, will make the healing process much quicker for your heart.

- **People Are Brought Into Our Lives For A Reason:**

The people who come into our lives are meant to be there for one reason or another. There really is no such thing as coincidence when it comes to the people that come and go in our lives. You need to remember that even though it is painful that your partner left, you likely learned valuable lessons about life and love. Everything in life is a learning experience and it is important that you pay attention to life's lessons.

- **Don't Fall Into The Bottomless Pit Of Your Mind:**

It is very important that you do not allow yourself to start thinking foolishly. By this I mean that it is not a good idea to sit around and think about if your ex is seeing other people or not. Do not sit around and wonder if you guys will ever get back together. This is a sure way to drive yourself crazy and you need to avoid it. Take things day by day and step by step and everything will work out the way it is supposed to.

- **Let Go Of Negative Feelings:**

You need to let go of all of your negative feelings and emotions, especially those of anger, hate, or plans of revenge. This will do absolutely no good for the process of healing your heart. On top of that, repairing your relationship will be next to impossible if you hold on to these feelings. Even if you do get back together, these feelings will eventually come back to the surface and destroy the relationship again. You must let go of these feelings!

- **Be Independent:**

When trying to heal your broken heart it is important that you learn to be independent once again. It will make you feel better when you realize that you are still capable of getting things done and although it may hurt that your partner is gone, life goes on. This will also be impressive to your ex and will heighten the chances of your love rekindling.

- **Seek Out Support:**

It is advised that you seek out support from friends and loved ones when trying to heal a broken heart. It is not a good idea for you to be alone constantly because you will likely just sit around and think about your ex. Go see a movie with a friend or go out to dinner with your family. You may be surprised by how much better it makes you feel.

- **Understand That You Can Be Loved**

You must understand that you are loveable. The fact that your relationship did not work out does not mean that it will not in the future or that you are a bad person. It just means that you need to work on some issues.

- **Build Your Self-Esteem:**

Building your self-esteem is a great way to help a person's heart in the healing process. When you feel good about yourself you will notice that you do not feel as much pain from the breakup and that you do not think about it as often as possible.

- **Keep In Mind Time Heals Everything:**

I know it hurts right now and it may seem as if the pain will never go away. However, the pain will subside and life will get brighter, you just have to give it some time. It is as the saying goes, time heals everything.

CHAPTER 2

UNDERSTAND WHAT WENT WRONG

Synopsis

If you plan on ever rekindling the love between you and your ex it is extremely important that you look over your relationship and discover what went wrong. This process is difficult for many people to do. It is important that you are honest with yourself during this process and that you consider the things you did wrong too. Trying to place all of the blame on your ex will get you nowhere.

The following chapter will go over the importance of understanding where things went wrong and will provide you with some examples of common problems that can rip a relationship apart. Continue reading if you are serious about winning back your ex because nothing will ever get better if the root of the problem is not fixed.

What Happened?

Now that you have come to terms with reality and have begun to heal your heart it is time for the next step in the process of trying to win back your ex's heart. It is time to look over your relationship and to discover where exactly things went wrong and what happened. Surely if you are trying to win your ex back there was some type of serious connection or else it would not be worth your efforts. There has to be a reason for why things took a turn for the worst. It is very likely that your relationship can be repaired; it is just going to take time and a lot of effort.

It is not advised that you skip the step of discovering where things went wrong, even if your ex wants to get back together immediately. Not addressing your issues and trying to just sweep them under the rug is a recipe for disaster. If you do not address the issues with your relationship any chances of a future attempt at making things work would surely be a waste of time. There is a reason why you have split ways and unless that issue is fixed it will surely end with the same results as before.

The hardest part of this process is probably going to be admitting your faults in the relationship and accepting responsibility for the things you could have done differently.

There was probably many times where your ex tried to explain their feelings to you about certain things and you did not pay them any attention. It is not too late to start working on these things.

Relationships are supposed to be give and take and both parties are supposed to contribute so it is important to think about if you were bring all you could to the table. At the same time it is not a good idea to sit around and dwell on the past. After you have discovered where things went wrong do not continue to sit around and think about it all day, take it for what it is and fix it.

Once you have discovered the issues with your relationship it is important that you begin trying to fix your wrong doing in the relationship. Think about all the conversations you and your ex had or the fights that you may have had and think about the things they were asking you to change. You need to begin fixing these things if you want a chance of winning back your ex. It may be hard to change some of your behaviors or habits but it is important that you do so. You must keep in mind however that it is important that you always remain true to who you are. You should not complete reinvent yourself you anyone but rather think about the things that make sense to change. The chances are if you do not like something about yourself, others will not appreciate it either.

This step may be difficult for you but it is extremely important. Do not try to rush things and fix all of your problems overnight because this will not happen! Take things slow and let love run its course.

CHAPTER 3

GETTING IN TOUCH AGAIN

Synopsis

Now that you have discovered where things went wrong and made changes to the things you could about yourself it is time to move on to the next step. It is now time to begin trying to get back in touch with your ex. You need to understand that it is extremely important that you are careful about how you approach this step in the process of winning back your ex because if it is not done correctly it can completely backfire. The last thing you want is to push your ex away even further and make all of the work you have done so far to try to win them back a complete waste.

The following chapter will provide you with some tips that you should seriously consider before trying to get back into contact with your ex. Remember, this step may take a while and it is important that you are not pushy. Let love work its magic and take your time, the reward will be well worth the wait when you have your ex in your arms once again.

Contact Your Ex

As mentioned before, it is now time that you should begin trying to contact your ex. This may be difficult for you to do and you may be scared to try and fix things because of fear of rejection. You need to keep in mind the fact that you will never get your ex back if you do not ever talk to them. It is time that you swallow your pride and reach out to them and let them know that you want to rekindle the spark you once had.

It is important that you go about this step in the right way. The following are eight simple to follow steps that will help you through this process and ensure that you have the best possible outcome.

- **Make The First Move:**

If you are serious about trying to get back with your ex it is important that you make the first move. In reality, you have no idea if your ex plans on ever contacting you again or ever trying to fix things between the two of you. That is why you must contact them first. It is important that you do not contact them before you are ready however because this will surely lead to undesired results. If your ex does not seem like they want to speak to you right away it is a good idea for you to give them some time and try again.

- **Don't Have Unrealistic Expectations:**

It is important when you contact your ex that you do not have unrealistic expectations of how the conversation will go. You should not expect to hear them say that everything is ok and that everything will go back to how it was immediately. These are completely unrealistic expectations because your ex is probably just as hurt as you are over the breakup. Things are going to take time to get better and you have to give your ex the time they need to heal as well.

Basically, you need to understand that your relationship is basically starting over.

- **Have A Good Attitude**

It is important that you are optimistic when contacting your ex. You do not want to fill your head with negative thoughts because they will surely get in the way of you rekindling your love with your ex. Have positive thoughts and believe in your heart that everything will work out and you will have a much better chance of succeeding.

- **Don't Over Do It:**

When contacting your ex and trying to fix your relationship you do not want to seem needy or bug your ex with a hundred phone calls throughout the day. As mentioned before, this is a process that is going to take time. Your ex will likely want a little bit of space at first. It is advised that you are proportional with the frequency of your calls.

- **Control Your Emotions:**

Before you even try to contact your ex it is important that you make sure that you have complete control of your emotions. You need to keep in mind that your ex may have some things to say that may be hard for you to hear. You need to be in an emotional state that will allow you to deal with this conversation in a productive manner.

Getting angry or upset when you contact your ex is a sure way of making sure you do not get back together.

- **Steer Clear Of The Past:**

It is important that you do not continuously revert your conversations back to the past. You need to discuss your issues in order to be able to fix them but you may want to wait a while before doing this. If you do discuss your issues in the past it is important that your statements are very well thought out and that you do not dwell in the past. Focus on the future and make it clear that you have the best of intentions for your relationship now. Describe to your ex the changes you have made and the person you plan on being now as well as the life that you can provide for them.

- **Don't Rush Them**

You should never rush or try to persuade your ex into getting back with you or coming back home. You need to let them decide when they are ready. You may want to bring the question up on if they think it would be a good idea but if they are not sure give them time and do not rush them.

- **Be Strong:**

You cannot give up to quickly when you are trying to contract your ex. If they do not want to speak to you at first do not give up but at the same time do not become a stalker. Your ex will surely appreciate your persistence and it will make them feel like they are worth something to you. Give them time and they will be sure to give you a chance.

Once you have contacted your ex and everything is going smoothly for a while it is time to try and arrange a face to face meeting. It is advised that you do not try and make the meeting somewhere private like at either of your houses. It is better that the meeting be in a public place like a coffee shop or a diner. This will make things more comfortable for both of you.

Make sure that you demonstrate the new you to your ex when you meet with them. Show them that you have done everything you can to acknowledge the needs and wants that were not met in the previous attempt at your relationship. The fact that you are trying will surely be noticed by your ex and will be much appreciated. It is important that just as on the phone you do not appear needy when you meet with your ex. Do not beg them to come back. Make it clear that you understand that things will take time and that you are willing to put forth the effort.

CHAPTER 4

IMPROVE COMMUNICATIONS

Synopsis

Once you have been talking for a while and both of you feel comfortable around one another it is time to start working on improving your communication skills with each other. It is important that the issues that split your relationship in the first place be resolved. It is also very important that people in a relationship are able to verbalize their feeling and thoughts in an appropriate manner. Just as the information should be relayed in an appropriate manner it needs to be received that way as well. So if you plan on giving your relationship another try it is highly advised that you work on your communication skills.

The following chapter will provide you with some helpful hints that will be sure to help you improve your communication skills and give your second shot more of a chance.

Learn How to Communicate

Communication is extremely important in any relationship, whether it be personal or social. That is why you need to work on your communication skills if you want things to work out with you and your ex. If you can talk your issues out with you ex they will surely be impressed and will be much more likely to give your relationship another chance.

The following are five steps you need to follow to ensure you are communicating in an effective manner.

- **Don't Interrupt**

It is important that you do not interrupt your ex when you are speaking with them. This can be very difficult to do at times, especially when emotions are involved or a problem is being discussed. You have to force yourself to stop speaking sometimes and to wait your turn. Your discussion will go nowhere if you are constantly interrupting your ex because neither one of you will ever make your point clear.

- **Make Sure You Listen:**

Just because you are not interrupting your ex and you can hear what they are saying does not mean that you are actually listening. You need to clear your mind of thoughts of what you will say next and make sure you are retaining what your ex says to you.

- **Be Honest And Have Open Discussions:**

It is important that you are always honest and that you are available to talk about anything. This will promote trust between you and your ex and make the chances of the two of you getting back together much greater. Lying to your ex and not being open to talk about certain things will surely make them feel like you have not changed and will make them feel as if giving it another try would be pointless. Always be honest!

- **Control Your Nonverbal Communication:**

A lot of people are not aware of the fact that they communicate more with nonverbal communication than they do with actual spoken words. There are certain things you should avoid when speaking to your ex is you want to have a productive conversation. For example, you should not have your arms crossed because this will give off the impression that you are closed to the conversation. You need to make sure that you are making eye contact as well and you need to respect space and boundaries.

- **Focus The Conversation On the Present:**

It is important that you do not let your conversations constantly shift back to past issues, especially those that have been resolved. If you do not let go of the past you will find yourself in an endless cycle that will get you nowhere and will surely not contribute to you getting back together with your ex. Some things are best just left alone and left in the past. Don't bring up old emotions and feelings that will damage your efforts. Problems need to be sorted out but not dwelled on.

If you follow these steps you will surely have productive conversations with your ex and you will be able to begin the process of repairing your damaged relationship. It may be hard at times to follow these rules while communicating with your ex but you must keep in mind that one day all of your efforts will likely be rewarded by you winning back the heart of your ex.

CHAPTER 5

THE HAPPY REUNION

Synopsis

Now that all of your efforts have paid off and it is time for the two of you to get back together there are some things you need to do. It is important that you make sure that you do not revert back to your old ways and that you do not let the relationship take the same turns that it did the last time when it did not work out. Keep in mind, just as easy as you have won your ex's heart back you could lose it again.

The following chapter will go over what to expect when you get back together with your ex as well as some tips that will help you keep the relationship together and ensure that your love for each other will last an eternity.

Together Again!

I am very happy for you and the fact that you have gotten back together with your ex and have stolen their heart back. Now you just need to make sure that you do not lose it again, especially because the chances of getting a third chance are very low. You need to make sure that you always keep in mind the way you felt when you lost partner and how bad it broke your heart. Do you want to go through that again? I didn't think so. You need to make sure that you steer clear of the actions and choices that contributed to the separation of the two of you last time. This will take time for you to master and you shouldn't expect your partner to have everything mastered straight away either.

There are certain things you can do to show your partner that you appreciate them and that you would do anything for them. There are also things you need to do that are vital for a successful and healthy relationship. A few examples are listed below.

- **Proper Communication:**

It is important that you have proper communication skills within a relationship if you want it to be successful and last. You need to know how to express to one another your thoughts and concerns without either one being offensive or being offended. This is easier said than done in the beginning but over time it becomes more and more easy. Practice proper communication skills whenever you get the chance and you will surely have the skill mastered in no time.

- **Learn Your Partner:**

You need to learn everything you can about your partner. This will show your partner that you are truly interested in them too and not just yourself. It will also make them feel appreciated and loved. The more you know about your partner the better. Learn their likes and dislikes. Learn what they are interested in and participate with them in these activates.

- **Express What You Need:**

You need to learn how to express what you need from the relationship in a healthy manner. People in relationships can fall into a pattern of expecting their significant other to be able to know what they are thinking or read their mind. This may be shocking news to some people but you cannot read minds. If you have a problem or you would like something to be addressed to need to make it understood to your partner. The hardest part of this is finding a way to do it in a positive manner but if you try hard enough you will find a way.

- **Do The Things You Did In The Early Time Of Your Relationship:**

It is important that you keep your relationship alive. Couples often times end up in a rut where they no longer go out and do the things they used to do. They may stop dressing up and lose the motivation to keep their selves up. It is important that you do the things you did in the early times of your relationship when your spark was alive.

Spending time with each other is very important but it is not good to sit around the house all of the time and never get out.

- **Have Passionate Sex:**

Sex is very important in a successful relationship. You need to make sure that you are satisfying the desires of your partner. Make sure you have discussions about each other's likes and dislikes. Make sure that you are not a selfish lover. Try making things special by laying out some flowers or drawing a bath with candles lit around it. There are many things you can do to make sex passionate and a true testament to love rather than just meaningless sex. Make sure you let your partner know that you love them and appreciate them and take the time to make sure they are satisfied.

Those were just a few of the countless tips there are for making sure that your relationship has the best chance possible to succeed. It may take time and effort but that is what relationships are about, give and take. If one person is taking too much and not giving enough there will surely be problems and things will eventually fall apart, again!

Wrapping Up

Winning back the heart of your ex is possible; it just may not be easy or happen overnight. If you use the information and helpful hints provided to you in this book you will have a much better chance. Once you do get your ex back it is extremely important that you both put in the needed amount of effort to keep everything going smoothly. A big part of the equation relates back to the golden rule we were all taught as a child, treat others the way we would like to be treated.

One thing that will surely motivate you to stay on the right track and make things work is to keep in mind the pain you went through when you lost ex in the first place. Once you get them back never let go because you do not know if you will get them back the next time.

I hope this book has been helpful for you and has provided you with some valuable information. Just believe that everything will work out and the power of love will make sure that it does.

Thank you for your time and I wish you the best of luck!

Printed by Libri Plureos GmbH in Hamburg,
Germany